THE UNBREAKABLE MARRIAGE

Gratitude Journal

THE UNBREAKABLE MARRIAGE: Gratitude Journal

Copyright © 2022 Jeeva & Sulojana Sam

ISBN: 978-1-7780861-4-4

All rights reserved. Except for brief excerpts for review purposes, no part of this book may be reproduced or used in any form or media without permission from the publisher.

Any website addresses recommended throughout this book are offered as a resource to you. These websites are not intended in any way to imply an endorsement from the authors, nor do they vouch for their content. The information in this book was correct at the time it was published.

All Scripture quotations, unless otherwise indicated, are taken from the Holy Bible, New International Version®, NIV®. Copyright ©1973, 1978, 1984, 2011 by Biblica, Inc.™ Used by permission of Zondervan. All rights reserved worldwide. www.zondervan.comThe "NIV" and "New International Version" are trademarks registered in the United States Patent and Trademark Office by Biblica, Inc.™

Scripture quotations marked NLT are taken from the Holy Bible, New Living Translation, copyright ©1996, 2004, 2015 by Tyndale House Foundation. Used by permission of Tyndale House Publishers, a Division of Tyndale House Ministries, Carol Stream, Illinois 60188. All rights reserved.

Scripture quotations marked TPT are from The Passion Translation®. Copyright © 2017, 2018 by Passion & Fire Ministries, Inc. Used by permission. All rights reserved. ThePassionTranslation.com.

Cover design by Hester Barnard. Graphic inspired by a vision God gave Steven Kasyanenko.
Typesetting by Krysta Koppel, Engage Communication Co.

Introduction

In the last decade, many books have been written on the power of gratitude. Scientific studies quoted in such publications as Psychology Today and Harvard Health Journal demonstrate that gratitude produces many benefits such as happiness, productivity, self-esteem, physical health, mental health, more satisfying relationships, and better sleep.[1] In our experience, gratitude is also an antidote to anxiety. A grateful spirit contributes greatly to a peaceful mind, and the peace inside of you will spill into what is outside of you, including your marriage!

Let us look at the spiritual significance of practicing gratitude on a regular basis. *"Enter His gates with thanksgiving and His courts with praise; give thanks to Him and bless His holy name"* (Psalm 100:4). While this is clearly an invitation to be thankful to God, we believe that the verse also implies that by expressing our gratitude to God, the doors are opened for us to enter His Presence. That is how powerful gratitude is! In our book *The Unbreakable Marriage*, we talk about 10 spiritual habits that sustain the habitation of the Holy Spirit. Gratitude is third on the list.

When you enter God's Presence with thanksgiving regularly, you are less likely to react to life's events out of your basic thoughts and feelings. By practicing thankfulness, you are preparing yourself to respond to everything that happens as one who reflects God's nature and character. Might that change the way you treat your spouse? We sure think so!

---

[1] https://www.psychologytoday.com/us/basics/gratitude ; https://www.health.harvard.edu/blog/in-praise-of-gratitude-201211215561

Here is how you can incorporate gratitude into your daily lives. In this Gratitude Journal, make two specific entries every day:

1. Ask yourself: **"What am I thankful for today?"** and write down your answer. You can do this either at the beginning of the day or the end of the day. You can be thankful for things as simple as the weather, a surprise phone call or message, your home, your health, your family, the green grass, a white blanket of snow, etc. Whatever strikes you as something you can be thankful for, write it down.

2. Ask yourself: **"What is one thing about my spouse that I am thankful for today?"** and write your answer. When you are in serious conflict (as you might be right now), you may not find it easy to find something to be thankful for in the moment. If that is the case, go back to the past and come up with something from your dating days or the earlier parts of your marriage. Go as far back as you need to and write down a reason for giving thanks. Here are some basic examples to get your memory going: That time he/she made breakfast for me; when he brushed the snow off my car; when we walked hand in hand from school; that surprise gift; his/her faithfulness in taking care of the laundry, etc.

The Apostle Paul tells us to "*Give thanks in all circumstances; for this is God's will for you in Christ Jesus*" (1 Thessalonians 5:18). Your current circumstances may not seem like they are reasons for gratitude, we understand that. These are the times when you need to look past what you see in the natural and tap into the spiritual realm. Enter into God's gates with thanksgiving!

Date: _____

What am I thankful for today?

_____

_____

_____

_____

_____

What is one thing about my spouse that I am thankful for today?

_____

_____

_____

*Give thanks in all circumstances;
for this is God's will for you in Christ Jesus.*
1 Thessalonians 5:18 (NIV)

Date: _____

What am I thankful for today?

_____

_____

_____

_____

_____

What is one thing about my spouse that I am thankful for today?

_____

_____

_____

Enter his gates with thanksgiving; go into his courts with praise. Give thanks to him and praise his name.
Psalm 100:4 (NLT)

Date: _____

What am I thankful for today?

_____

_____

_____

_____

_____

What is one thing about my spouse that I am thankful for today?

_____

_____

_____

Every time we pray for you our hearts overflow with thanksgiving to Father God, the Father of our Lord Jesus Christ.
Colossians 1:3 (TPT)

Date: _____

What am I thankful for today?

_____

_____

_____

_____

_____

What is one thing about my spouse that I am thankful for today?

_____

_____

_____

"Gratitude is also an antidote to anxiety."
Jeeva and Sulojana Sam

Date: _____

What am I thankful for today?

_____

_____

_____

_____

_____

What is one thing about my spouse that I am thankful for today?

_____

_____

_____

*Now, our God, we give you thanks,
and praise your glorious name.*
1 Chronicles 29:13 (NIV)

Date: _____

What am I thankful for today?

_____

_____

_____

_____

_____

What is one thing about my spouse that I am thankful for today?

_____

_____

_____

Don't be pulled in different directions or worried about a thing. Be saturated in prayer throughout each day, offering your faith-filled requests before God with overflowing gratitude...

Date: _____

What am I thankful for today?

_____

_____

_____

_____

_____

_____

What is one thing about my spouse that I am thankful for today?

_____

_____

_____

...Tell him every detail of your life, then God's wonderful peace that transcends human understanding, will guard your heart and mind through Jesus Christ. Philippians 4:6-7 (TPT)

Date: _____

What am I thankful for today?

_____

_____

_____

_____

_____

What is one thing about my spouse that I am thankful for today?

_____

_____

_____

*I will give thanks to the LORD because of his righteousness;
I will sing the praises of the name of the LORD Most High.*
Psalm 7:17 (NIV)

Date: _____

What am I thankful for today?

_____

_____

_____

_____

_____

What is one thing about my spouse that I am thankful for today?

_____

_____

_____

For everything God created is good, and nothing is to be rejected if it is received with thanksgiving,
1 Timothy 4:4 (NIV)

Date: _____

What am I thankful for today?

_____

_____

_____

_____

_____

What is one thing about my spouse that I am thankful for today?

_____

_____

_____

"Your current circumstances may not seem like they are reasons for gratitude, we understand that...

Date: _____

What am I thankful for today?

_____

_____

_____

_____

_____

What is one thing about my spouse that I am thankful for today?

_____

_____

_____

...these are the times when you need to look past what you see in the natural and tap into the spiritual realm."
Jeeva and Sulojana Sam

Date: _____

What am I thankful for today?

_____

_____

_____

_____

_____

What is one thing about my spouse that I am thankful for today?

_____

_____

_____

We always have to thank God for you, brothers and sisters,
for you are dearly loved by the Lord.
He proved it by choosing you…

Date: _____

What am I thankful for today?

_____

_____

_____

_____

_____

What is one thing about my spouse that I am thankful for today?

_____

_____

_____

...from the beginning for salvation through the Spirit, who set you apart for holiness, and through your belief in the truth.
2 Thessalonians 2:13 (TPT)

Date: _____

What am I thankful for today?

_____

_____

_____

_____

_____

What is one thing about my spouse that I am thankful for today?

_____

_____

_____

*Keep on giving your thanks to God, for he is so good!
His constant, tender love lasts forever!*
Psalm 118:1 (TPT)

Date: _____

What am I thankful for today?

_____

_____

_____

_____

_____

What is one thing about my spouse that I am thankful for today?

_____

_____

_____

Make thankfulness your sacrifice to God, and keep the vows you made to the Most High.
Psalm 50:14 (NLT)

Date: _____

What am I thankful for today?

_____

_____

_____

_____

_____

What is one thing about my spouse that I am thankful for today?

_____

_____

_____

Therefore, since we are receiving a kingdom that cannot be shaken, let us be thankful...

Date: _____

What am I thankful for today?

_____

_____

_____

_____

_____

What is one thing about my spouse that I am thankful for today?

_____

_____

_____

...and so worship God acceptably with reverence and awe,
Hebrews 12:28 (NIV)

Date: _____

What am I thankful for today?

_____

_____

_____

_____

_____

What is one thing about my spouse that I am thankful for today?

_____

_____

_____

Amen! Praise and glory and wisdom and thanks and honour and power and strength be to our God for ever and ever. Amen!
Revelation 7:12 (NIV)

Date: _____

What am I thankful for today?

_____

_____

_____

_____

_____

What is one thing about my spouse that I am thankful for today?

_____

_____

_____

Always give thanks to Father God for every person he brings into your life in the name of our Lord Jesus Christ.
Ephesians 5:20 (TPT)

Date: _____

What am I thankful for today?

_____

_____

_____

_____

_____

What is one thing about my spouse that I am thankful for today?

_____

_____

_____

Time to share your journal entries with your spouse.
Use the steps on the next page to share and reflect.

SHARE YOUR GRATITUDE JOURNAL

Take time to share with each other every answer you have written to the question: **"What is one thing about my spouse that I am thankful for today?"** Look each other in the eye as much as possible during this sharing.

One spouse begins by reading all the reasons from their journal. Then the other spouse shares all their entries. Overwhelm each other with gratitude.

You can weave them into a prayer at the end, if you would like, such as,

"Lord, I thank you for _____.

I thank you that he/she _____."

How did your spouse respond to what you shared? How did that make you feel? Share with them any entries that particularly delighted or surprised you.

_____

_____

How did it make you feel to hear all the reasons for which your spouse is grateful for you? Share with them any entries that particularly delighted or surprised you.

_____

_____

Note: If you are using The Unbreakable Marriage Workbook, you can enter these responses there as well. Bookmark this page for future reference.

Date: _____

What am I thankful for today?

_____

_____

_____

_____

_____

What is one thing about my spouse that I am thankful for today?

_____

_____

_____

*Be faithful to pray as intercessors who are fully alert
and giving thanks to God.*
Colossians 4:2 (TPT)

Date: _____

What am I thankful for today?

_____

_____

_____

_____

_____

What is one thing about my spouse that I am thankful for today?

_____

_____

_____

We praise you, God, we praise you, for your Name is near;
people tell of your wonderful deeds.
Psalm 75:1 (NIV)

Date: _____

What am I thankful for today?

_____

_____

_____

_____

_____

What is one thing about my spouse that I am thankful for today?

_____

_____

_____

I am always thanking my God for you because he has given you such free and open access to his grace through your union with Jesus, the Messiah. 1 Corinthians 1:4 (TPT)

Date: _____

What am I thankful for today?

_____

_____

_____

_____

_____

What is one thing about my spouse that I am thankful for today?

_____

_____

_____

"A grateful spirit contributes greatly to a peaceful mind...

Date: _____

What am I thankful for today?

_____

_____

_____

_____

_____

What is one thing about my spouse that I am thankful for today?

_____

_____

_____

...and the peace inside of you will spill into what is outside of you, including your marriage."
Jeeva and Sulojana Sam

Date: _____

What am I thankful for today?

_____

_____

_____

_____

_____

_____

What is one thing about my spouse that I am thankful for today?

_____

_____

_____

*Let them sacrifice thank offerings
and tell of his works with songs of joy.*
Psalm 107:22 (NIV)

Date: _____

What am I thankful for today?

_____

_____

_____

_____

_____

What is one thing about my spouse that I am thankful for today?

_____

_____

_____

*I thank my God every time I remember you.
In all my prayers for all of you, I always pray with joy…*
Philippians 1:3-4 (NIV)

Date: _____

What am I thankful for today?

_____

_____

_____

_____

_____

What is one thing about my spouse that I am thankful for today?

_____

_____

_____

Let every activity of your lives and every word that comes from your lips be drenched with the beauty of our Lord Jesus, the Anointed One…

Date: _____

What am I thankful for today?

_____

_____

_____

_____

_____

_____

What is one thing about my spouse that I am thankful for today?

_____

_____

_____

...And bring your constant praise to God the Father because of what Christ has done for you!
Colossians 3:17 (TPT)

Date: _____

What am I thankful for today?

_____

_____

_____

_____

_____

What is one thing about my spouse that I am thankful for today?

_____

_____

_____

*Sing out with songs of thanksgiving to the Lord!
Let's sing our praises with melodies overflowing!*
Psalm 147:7 (TPT)

Date: _____

What am I thankful for today?

_____

_____

_____

_____

_____

What is one thing about my spouse that I am thankful for today?

_____

_____

_____

All this is for your benefit, so that the grace that is reaching more and more people may cause thanksgiving to overflow to the glory of God. 2 Corinthians 4:15 (NIV)

Date: _____

What am I thankful for today?

_____

_____

_____

_____

_____

What is one thing about my spouse that I am thankful for today?

_____

_____

_____

You can pass through his open gates with the password of praise.
Come right into his presence with thanksgiving...

Date: _____

What am I thankful for today?

_____

_____

_____

_____

_____

What is one thing about my spouse that I am thankful for today?

_____

_____

_____

*...Come bring your thank offering to him
and affectionately bless his beautiful name!*
Psalm 100:4 (TPT)

Date: _____

What am I thankful for today?

_____

_____

_____

_____

_____

_____

What is one thing about my spouse that I am thankful for today?

_____

_____

_____

But we ought always to thank God for you, brothers and sisters loved by the Lord, because God chose you as firstfruits...
2 Thessalonians 2:13a (NIV)

Date: _____

What am I thankful for today?

_____

_____

_____

_____

_____

What is one thing about my spouse that I am thankful for today?

_____

_____

_____

Bring your praise as an offering and your thanks as a sacrifice as you sing your story of miracles with a joyful song.
Psalm 107:22 (TPT)

Date: _____

What am I thankful for today?

_____

_____

_____

_____

_____

What is one thing about my spouse that I am thankful for today?

_____

_____

_____

*First, I thank my God through Jesus Christ for all of you,
because your faith is being reported all over the world.*
Romans 1:8 (NIV)

Date: _____

What am I thankful for today?

_____

_____

_____

_____

_____

What is one thing about my spouse that I am thankful for today?

_____

_____

_____

"By expressing our gratitude to God, the doors are opened for us to enter His presence."
Jeeva and Sulojana Sam

Date: _____

What am I thankful for today?

_____

_____

_____

_____

_____

What is one thing about my spouse that I am thankful for today?

_____

_____

_____

God, our hearts spill over with praise to you! We overflow with thanks, for your name is the "Near One..."

Date: _____

What am I thankful for today?

_____

_____

_____

_____

_____

What is one thing about my spouse that I am thankful for today?

_____

_____

_____

...All we want to talk about is your wonderful works!
Psalm 75:1 (TPT)

Date: _____

What am I thankful for today?

_____

_____

_____

_____

_____

What is one thing about my spouse that I am thankful for today?

_____

_____

_____

*Time to share your journal entries with your spouse.
Use the steps from page 25 to share and reflect.*

Date: _____

What am I thankful for today?

_____

_____

_____

_____

_____

What is one thing about my spouse that I am thankful for today?

_____

_____

_____

Devote yourselves to prayer, being watchful and thankful.
Colossians 4:2 (NIV)

Date: _____

What am I thankful for today?

_____

_____

_____

_____

_____

What is one thing about my spouse that I am thankful for today?

_____

_____

_____

*"We give thanks to you, Lord God Almighty,
who is, and who was…*

Date: _____

What am I thankful for today?

_____

_____

_____

_____

_____

What is one thing about my spouse that I am thankful for today?

_____

_____

_____

...because you have established your great and limitless power and begun to reign!
Revelation 11:7 (TPT)

Date: _____

What am I thankful for today?

_____

_____

_____

_____

_____

What is one thing about my spouse that I am thankful for today?

_____

_____

_____

Give thanks to the LORD, for he is good;
his love endures forever.
Psalm 118:1 (NIV)

Date: _____

What am I thankful for today?

_____

_____

_____

_____

_____

What is one thing about my spouse that I am thankful for today?

_____

_____

_____

"Gratitude changes our awareness of God's closeness and goodness."
Jeeva and Sulojana Sam

Date: _____

What am I thankful for today?

_____

_____

_____

_____

_____

What is one thing about my spouse that I am thankful for today?

_____

_____

_____

*Don't worry about anything; instead, pray about everything.
Tell God what you need, and thank him for all he has done.*
Philippians 4:6 (NLT)

Date: _____

What am I thankful for today?

_____

_____

_____

_____

_____

What is one thing about my spouse that I am thankful for today?

_____

_____

_____

We always thank God, the Father of our Lord Jesus Christ, when we pray for you…
Colossians 1:3 (NIV)

Date: _____

What am I thankful for today?

_____

_____

_____

_____

_____

What is one thing about my spouse that I am thankful for today?

_____

_____

_____

*Everyone come meet his face with a thankful heart.
Don't hold back your praises...*

Date: _____

What am I thankful for today?

_____

_____

_____

_____

_____

What is one thing about my spouse that I am thankful for today?

_____

_____

_____

...make him great by your shouts of joy!
Psalm 95:2 (TPT)

Date: _____

What am I thankful for today?

_____

_____

_____

_____

_____

What is one thing about my spouse that I am thankful for today?

_____

_____

_____

*I always thank my God for you because of
his grace given you in Christ Jesus.*
1 Corinthians 1:4 (NIV)

Date: _____

What am I thankful for today?

_____

_____

_____

_____

_____

What is one thing about my spouse that I am thankful for today?

_____

_____

_____

And in the midst of everything be always giving thanks, for this is God's perfect plan for you in Christ Jesus.
1 Thessalonians 5:18 (TPT)

Date: _____

What am I thankful for today?

_____

_____

_____

_____

_____

What is one thing about my spouse that I am thankful for today?

_____

_____

_____

*Since we are receiving our rights to an unshakable kingdom
we should be extremely thankful...*

Date: _____

What am I thankful for today?

_____

_____

_____

_____

_____

What is one thing about my spouse that I am thankful for today?

_____

_____

_____

...and offer God the purest worship that delights his heart as we lay down our lives in absolute surrender, filled with awe.
Hebrews 12:28 (TPT)

Date: _____

What am I thankful for today?

_____

_____

_____

_____

_____

What is one thing about my spouse that I am thankful for today?

_____

_____

_____

*Yahweh is my strength and my wraparound shield.
When I fully trust in you, help is on the way…*

Date: _____

What am I thankful for today?

_____

_____

_____

_____

_____

What is one thing about my spouse that I am thankful for today?

_____

_____

_____

*...I jump for joy and burst forth with ecstatic, passionate praise!
I will sing songs of what you mean to me!*
Psalm 28:7 (TPT)

Date: _____

What am I thankful for today?

_____

_____

_____

_____

_____

What is one thing about my spouse that I am thankful for today?

_____

_____

_____

Let the message of Christ dwell among you richly as you teach and admonish one another with all wisdom…

Date: _____

What am I thankful for today?

_____

_____

_____

_____

_____

What is one thing about my spouse that I am thankful for today?

_____

_____

_____

...through psalms, hymns, and songs from the Spirit, singing to God with gratitude in your hearts.
Colossians 3:16 (NIV)

Date: _____

What am I thankful for today?

_____

_____

_____

_____

_____

What is one thing about my spouse that I am thankful for today?

_____

_____

_____

And whatever you do, whether in word or deed, do it all in the name of the Lord Jesus, giving thanks to God the Father through him. Colossians 3:17 (NIV)

Date: _____

What am I thankful for today?

_____

_____

_____

_____

_____

What is one thing about my spouse that I am thankful for today?

_____

_____

_____

"Gratitude produces many benefits such as happiness, productivity, self-esteem, physical health, mental health, more satisfying relationships, and better sleep." Jeeva and Sulojana Sam

Date: _____

What am I thankful for today?

_____

_____

_____

_____

_____

What is one thing about my spouse that I am thankful for today?

_____

_____

_____

*Time to share your journal entries with your spouse.
Use the steps from page 25 to share and reflect.*

Date: _____

What am I thankful for today?

_____

_____

_____

_____

_____

What is one thing about my spouse that I am thankful for today?

_____

_____

_____

"We give thanks to you, Lord God Almighty, the One who is and who was, because you have taken your great power and have begun to reign." Revelation 11:17 (NIV)

Date: _____

What am I thankful for today?

_____

_____

_____

_____

_____

What is one thing about my spouse that I am thankful for today?

_____

_____

_____

And give thanks for everything to God the Father in the name of our Lord Jesus Christ.
Ephesians 5:20 (NLT)

Date: _____

What am I thankful for today?

_____

_____

_____

_____

_____

What is one thing about my spouse that I am thankful for today?

_____

_____

_____

*We know that all creation is beautiful to God and there is
nothing to be refused if it is received with gratitude.*
1 Timothy 4:4 (TPT)

Date: _____

What am I thankful for today?

_____

_____

_____

_____

_____

What is one thing about my spouse that I am thankful for today?

_____

_____

_____

*I will worship you, Yahweh, with extended hands
as my whole heart erupts with praise...*

Date: _____

What am I thankful for today?

_____

_____

_____

_____

_____

What is one thing about my spouse that I am thankful for today?

_____

_____

_____

*...I will tell everyone everywhere
about your wonderful works!*
Psalm 9:1 (TPT)

Date: _____

What am I thankful for today?

_____

_____

_____

_____

_____

What is one thing about my spouse that I am thankful for today?

_____

_____

_____

*"By practicing thankfulness,
you are preparing yourself to respond…*

Date: _____

What am I thankful for today?

_____

_____

_____

_____

_____

What is one thing about my spouse that I am thankful for today?

_____

_____

_____

*...to everything that happens as one who reflects
God's nature and character."*
Jeeva and Sulojana Sam

Date: _____

What am I thankful for today?

_____

_____

_____

_____

_____

What is one thing about my spouse that I am thankful for today?

_____

_____

_____

*When I come to your altar, Yahweh,
I'll be clean before you...*

Date: _____

What am I thankful for today?

_____

_____

_____

_____

_____

What is one thing about my spouse that I am thankful for today?

_____

_____

_____

...approaching with songs of thanksgiving,
singing songs of your mighty miracles.
Psalm 26:6-7 (TPT)

Date: _____

What am I thankful for today?

_____

_____

_____

_____

_____

What is one thing about my spouse that I am thankful for today?

_____

_____

_____

My prayers for you are full of praise to God as I give him thanks for you with great joy! I'm so grateful for our union...
Philippians 1:3-4 (TPT)

Date: _____

What am I thankful for today?

_____

_____

_____

_____

_____

What is one thing about my spouse that I am thankful for today?

_____

_____

_____

*From them will come songs of thanksgiving
and the sound of rejoicing.*
Jeremiah 30:19a (NIV)

Date: _____

What am I thankful for today?

_____

_____

_____

_____

_____

What is one thing about my spouse that I am thankful for today?

_____

_____

_____

Every spiritual blessing in the heavenly realm has already been lavished upon us as a love gift from our wonderful heavenly Father, the Father of our Lord Jesus...

Date: _____

What am I thankful for today?

_____

_____

_____

_____

_____

What is one thing about my spouse that I am thankful for today?

_____

_____

_____

…all because he sees us wrapped into Christ. This is why we celebrate him with all our hearts!
Ephesians 1:3 (TPT)

Date: _____

What am I thankful for today?

_____

_____

_____

_____

_____

What is one thing about my spouse that I am thankful for today?

_____

_____

_____

"Amen! Praise and glory, wisdom and thanksgiving, honour, power, and might belong to our God forever and ever! Amen!" Revelation 7:12 (TPT)

Date: _____

What am I thankful for today?

_____

_____

_____

_____

_____

What is one thing about my spouse that I am thankful for today?

_____

_____

_____

*Return to your rest, my soul, for the LORD
has been good to you.*
Psalm 116:7 (NIV)

Date: _____

What am I thankful for today?

_____

_____

_____

_____

_____

What is one thing about my spouse that I am thankful for today?

_____

_____

_____

I give thanks to God for all of you, because the testimony of your faith is spreading throughout the world.
Romans 1:8 (TPT)

Date: _____

What am I thankful for today?

_____

_____

_____

_____

_____

What is one thing about my spouse that I am thankful for today?

_____

_____

_____

*Praise God for his astonishing gift,
which is far too great for words!*
2 Corinthians 9:15 (TPT)

Date: _____

What am I thankful for today?

_____

_____

_____

_____

_____

What is one thing about my spouse that I am thankful for today?

_____

_____

_____

So then, just as you received Christ Jesus as Lord, continue to live your lives in him, rooted and built up in him…

Date: _____

What am I thankful for today?

_____

_____

_____

_____

_____

What is one thing about my spouse that I am thankful for today?

_____

_____

_____

...strengthened in the faith as you were taught, and overflowing with thankfulness.
Colossians 2:6-7 (NIV)

Date: _____

What am I thankful for today?

_____

_____

_____

_____

_____

What is one thing about my spouse that I am thankful for today?

_____

_____

_____

*Time to share your journal entries with your spouse.
Use the steps from page 25 to share and reflect.*

Date: _____

What am I thankful for today?

_____

_____

_____

_____

_____

What is one thing about my spouse that I am thankful for today?

_____

_____

_____

*But I will give my thanks to you, Yahweh,
for you make everything right in the end...*

Date: _____

What am I thankful for today?

_____

_____

_____

_____

_____

What is one thing about my spouse that I am thankful for today?

_____

_____

_____

I will sing my highest praise to the God of the Highest Place!
Psalm 7:17 (TPT)

Date: _____

What am I thankful for today?

_____

_____

_____

_____

_____

What is one thing about my spouse that I am thankful for today?

_____

_____

_____

Every time I think of you, I give thanks to my God.
Philippians 1:3 (NLT)

Date: _____

What am I thankful for today?

_____

_____

_____

_____

_____

What is one thing about my spouse that I am thankful for today?

_____

_____

_____

*The LORD is my strength and my shield;
my heart trusts in him, and he helps me...*

Date: _____

What am I thankful for today?

_____

_____

_____

_____

_____

What is one thing about my spouse that I am thankful for today?

_____

_____

_____

...My heart leaps for joy, and with my song I praise him.
Psalm 28:7 (NIV)

Date: _____

What am I thankful for today?

_____

_____

_____

_____

_____

What is one thing about my spouse that I am thankful for today?

_____

_____

_____

Thanks be to God for his indescribable gift!
2 Corinthians 9:15 (NIV)

Date: _____

What am I thankful for today?

_____

_____

_____

_____

_____

What is one thing about my spouse that I am thankful for today?

_____

_____

_____

*We are grateful to God for your lives
and we always pray for you.*
1 Thessalonians 1:2 (TPT)

Date: _____

What am I thankful for today?

_____

_____

_____

_____

_____

What is one thing about my spouse that I am thankful for today?

_____

_____

_____

*Let us come before him with thanksgiving
and extol him with music and song.*
Psalm 95:2 (NIV)

Date: _____

What am I thankful for today?

_____

_____

_____

_____

_____

What is one thing about my spouse that I am thankful for today?

_____

_____

_____

I thank and praise you, God of my ancestors:
You have given me wisdom and power...
Daniel 2:23a (NIV)

Date: _____

What am I thankful for today?

_____

_____

_____

_____

_____

What is one thing about my spouse that I am thankful for today?

_____

_____

_____

*Let my soul be at rest again,
for the LORD has been good to me.*
Psalm 116:7 (NLT)

Date: _____

What am I thankful for today?

_____

_____

_____

_____

_____

What is one thing about my spouse that I am thankful for today?

_____

_____

_____

*Enter his gates with thanksgiving, and his courts with praise;
Give thanks to him; bless his name.*
Psalm 100:4 (NIV)

Date: _____

What am I thankful for today?

_____

_____

_____

_____

_____

What is one thing about my spouse that I am thankful for today?

_____

_____

_____

Yes, all things work for your enrichment so that more of God's marvelous grace will spread to more and more people...

Date: _____

What am I thankful for today?

_____

_____

_____

_____

_____

What is one thing about my spouse that I am thankful for today?

_____

_____

_____

*...resulting in an even greater increase of praise to God,
bringing him even more glory!*
2 Corinthians 4:15 (TPT)

Date: _____

What am I thankful for today?

_____

_____

_____

_____

_____

What is one thing about my spouse that I am thankful for today?

_____

_____

_____

*Let your roots grow down into him,
and let your lives be built on him...*

Date: _____

What am I thankful for today?

_____

_____

_____

_____

_____

What is one thing about my spouse that I am thankful for today?

_____

_____

_____

...Then your faith will grow strong in the truth you were taught, and you will overflow with thankfulness.
Colossians 2:7 (NLT)

Date: _____

What am I thankful for today?

_____

_____

_____

_____

_____

What is one thing about my spouse that I am thankful for today?

_____

_____

_____

Do not be anxious about anything, but in every situation, by prayer and petition, with thanksgiving, present your requests to God...

Date: _____

What am I thankful for today?

_____

_____

_____

_____

_____

What is one thing about my spouse that I am thankful for today?

_____

_____

_____

...And the peace of God, which transcends all understanding, will guard your hearts and your minds in Christ Jesus. Philippians 4:6-7 (NIV)

Date: _____

What am I thankful for today?

_____

_____

_____

_____

_____

What is one thing about my spouse that I am thankful for today?

_____

_____

_____

*Proclaiming aloud your praise
and telling of all your wonderful deeds.*
Psalm 26:7 (NIV)

Date: _____

What am I thankful for today?

_____

_____

_____

_____

_____

What is one thing about my spouse that I am thankful for today?

_____

_____

_____

Praise be to the God and Father of our Lord Jesus Christ, who has blessed us in the heavenly realms with every spiritual blessing in Christ. Ephesians 1:3 (NIV)

Date: _____

What am I thankful for today?

_____

_____

_____

_____

_____

What is one thing about my spouse that I am thankful for today?

_____

_____

_____

Time to share your journal entries with your spouse.
Use the steps from page 25 to share and reflect.

Afterword:
Where Do We Go From Here?

Congratulations on working your way through this Gratitude Journal! This is just one step in moving towards breakthrough in your marriage. Perhaps you feel like you have just scratched the surface and are looking for more assistance to experience a full breakthrough.

If that's you, we would highly recommend that you receive personal, customized mentorship with us or another mentoring couple we have trained, over 12 weeks. This includes weekly sessions, mid-week checkups, unlimited inner healing sessions and 24/7 access to your mentors via email and text. 3 monthly follow-ups thereafter are also included. Results guaranteed or money back (conditions apply). By application only at www.thesams.ca.

We invite all of you to join our free Facebook group "The Unbreakable Marriage Community" where you can interact with other readers of this book and encourage one another. We will also be posting more teachings, updates and information on events you can attend to take your marriage to greater heights in that group.

Just click on:
http://www.facebook.com/groups/theunbreakablemarriage/
or scan the barcode below:

You can also reach Jeeva & Sulojana by e-mail: theunbreakablemarriage@gmail.com.
Connect with them on social media:
Facebook: @theunbreakablemarriagebook
Instagram: @theunbreakablemarriage

www.ingramcontent.com/pod-product-compliance
Lightning Source LLC
Chambersburg PA
CBHW072102110526
44590CB00018B/3282